Resume Writ
The Ultimate, Most Up-
to-date Guide to
Writing a Resume that
Lands YOU the Job!

Get Hired Today!

A.J. Robbins

Author's Note

First I want to thank you and congratulate you for downloading Resume Writing 2016.
This book contains proven steps and strategies on how to write a truly magnificent resume that will inevitably ensure you a job interview.

Here's an inescapable fact: if you wish to succeed in modern society and get the job you desire and deserve you will have to face fierce competition. Bear in mind that the job position you want to apply for will probably attract between 100 and 1000 applicants, so your resume has to show that among all of them that You are the person that employer needs!

The truth is that it doesn't really matter if you are the most perfect candidate in the whole wide world for the job, if you don't know how to promote yourself you will not be hired. That's what a resume is all about - advertising your skills and qualifications. Do you know that people more often tend to buy the best advertised product than the best product itself? So, if you wish to be one in a thousand that will get that interview call, no matter what your profession is, you will have to learn to write strong, but subtle, advertising copy.

This book is here to guide you through the essential steps of writing a masterpiece of a resume. It will teach you some basics regarding the knowledge of how a spectacular resume should look like, what it's supposed to contain and what you need to avoid.

It's time for you to write a breathtaking resume and make those dreams come true!

Table of Contents

Chapter 1: Technicalities

Your resume is your business card for the new potential employer. You want to present an appearance of neatness, efficiency, and professionalism. To best make use of your 30 second introduction, the following tips will help you design and draft an eye-catching and easily discerned resume.

What is a Resume?

A resume is a marketing tool that has only one specific purpose: to get you an interview. A resume is not a biography; it's not supposed to tell a story about your employment experience with every single job or task, or to present your career in its entirety. A resume is just an advertisement. If you manage to look at it your personal advertising tool, you will do a perfect job when writing one. I will tell you about preferred length of your resume later on, but for now I want you to think about that short form exploding commercial that will make your abilities look beneficial to the potential employer.

Length of a Resume

There is no set length for a resume. If you look up and read some examples you will see that they are 1 to 3 pages long, and you can find both perfect ones and the worst ones in that 1 to 3 scale, so let me rephrase that opening line: there is no set length for a good resume.

Don't get confused if someone tells you that your resume should be limited to one page that was the golden rule for writing a resume twenty years ago. That pattern is now broken and the ideal length is one that will represent your qualities in the best possible manner, but that won't be boring or full of phrases that don't mean anything.

You have to find the perfect balance so that you don't omit any valuable information, but also not to make it look stretched and overflowing with meaningless data. Don't struggle to enhance that one extra page in the hope you'll look more qualified in the eyes of the potential employer. You don't need to write about past experiences that don't enhance your current goal. Stay focused on presenting your qualities that are relevant to a specific job. Every word in the resume should sell you to a possible employer. In addition, if you want to get your employer's attention and win the job interview, you should also leave some mystery about you for the interview.

Although only you can ultimately decide on the perfect length for your resume I want to give you a few tips that could help you make that decision.

If you have less than 8 years of experience, or you are pursuing a profound career change, so that your previous experience isn't relevant for your new job, you should write a one-page resume.

If you have 8 or more years of experience related to your goal, or your field requires a great set of skills that need to be delineated to prove your education and knowledge, consider writing a two-page resume. In that case make sure that you put the most relevant information at the top of the first page.

You should write a longer resume, if you are, let's say, a C-level executive with a large array of leadership accomplishments, or you wish to get a job in an academic or scientific field, and must provide a list of publications, licenses, professional courses or patents.

Look of a Resume

When you start writing your resume you need to try to put yourself in the headspace of the person to whom it is going. Think about how you would feel reading your resume and what kind of resumes you would like to see, what would manage to draw your attention, what would upset you, what would annoy you.

Now, because it's obvious you don't want to annoy your potential employer, let's talk about how you resume should be made.

You want your resume to be easy to read, so in order not to make it graphically confusing you shouldn't use more than two fonts. Additionally, you want to avoid fancy creative borders, tables, images and text boxes. So, get rid of anything that's not relevant and is derived of great attention drawing potential. Keep it clean and simple.

The first reading of a resume is basically a quick 20 second scanning of a page, in those 20 seconds your employer could make the biggest mistake of his life by putting your resume on the discard pile. The best way to avoid that from happening is to make your resume easy to scan. Bold all resume headings, titles and important data, also you should use bullets rather than paragraphs when listing crucial information. This is a set of rules you need to follow when sending an application. The majority of companies have moved toward digital systems and scanning software in order to review applications more quickly, called Applicant Tracking Systems (ATS). Those systems are programmed mostly to search for keywords and phrases that are relevant for that specific position.

When writing a resume look at the keywords included in job postings and incorporate them into your application, making sure that you include most of them to increase your chances of passing that initial round of scanning. Don't forget that some of ATSs are programmed to read pdf files, and for some MS Word. So when sending your resume, scan the advertisement for a preferred file format.

In addition to this chapter, I wish to give you a few more simple tips that will help you beat the Applicant Tracking System (Note: if you are inexperienced reader and not familiar with all the terms stated here it would be best for you to return to this section after reading chapters 2 and 3.):

1. Use standard resume headings. Whether you call it "Professional Summary" or "Career Summary," or "Work Experience" sticking to these standard headings is best way to go. If you try to over-customize your resume heading, chances are it won't do anything good, but instead the opposite. ATSs are typically unable to recognize nonstandard headings, so by using them you are risking your resume being rejected even before somebody actually reads it.

2. Don't edit headers and footers. ATSs are usually not able to read headers and footers so it's not a good idea to put important information there. It would be the

best if you don't write anything there actually; headers and footers are best left empty with standard 1-inch margins.

3. Use appropriate keywords. When reading a job proposal search for keywords included there and use them; ATS will look for them in your resume. However, be aware that simply using any form of these keywords will not be enough. Keywords must be formatted to echo the original job description exactly so as to match the ATS criteria; there is a huge difference between "Microsoft Word" and "MS Word".

4. Left alignment and conservative typeface. Use left alignment for when formatting your resume text. Centering of text or block text and right text alignment is not acceptable by the ATS and it will cruelly discard your resume. Also use only the most conservative typeface (Arial, Helvetica, Georgia, Calibri, or Garamond). Times New Roman is considered boring and old fashioned.

5. Don't include any acronyms. ATSs won't understand any acronyms, even those that are well known like BMW. If you wish to include acronyms on your resume you need to spell it first so that scanning software is able to read it.

6. Don't make any spelling mistakes. This is something you should be aware of even when sending a physical application. ATS won't be able to read a word if it isn't spelled correctly, the hiring manager will be, but it's certain that your application won't pass the first round of reading anyway. Resumes with spelling or grammar errors will be rejected automatically.

Chapter 2: Resume Formats

Now that you have the technical knowledge you need in order to write a spectacular resume, we will move on to the next step - resume formats. There are two basic types of resumes: chronological and functional. There is also a third that is a combination of chronological and functional formats and it's called, you'll never guess, a combined resume.

Each resume format has their own set of advantages and naturally, disadvantages, so you should choose the style that reflects your goals and unique background. I will help you determine which one to choose by presenting each style and listing their pros and cons. We'll discuss in detail in which order sections should be organized and each of them will be described in detail in the next chapter of the book.

Chronological Resume

The first format I wish to talk about is the chronological, since it's most commonly used by the job seekers. This style was probably your first thought when you heard the phrase "resume format". When writing your resume in the chronological style, your main focus should be on the experience section. You will describe each job in moderate detail and will not focus on skills or accomplishments at the beginning.

When listing your work experience information, you should start with the most recent job you've had and make your way to the oldest (because of the order this style is sometimes called reverse-chronological format). The main reason this format is preferred by job seekers is because it accommodates all industries and levels of experience. Do bear in mind, however, that it's not the best option for someone making a career change.

This structure is mostly used when you are staying in the same profession, since chronologically listed job experiences are a good way of demonstrating a vertical career progression.

The disadvantage for this formatting type is that it's really difficult to highlight what you do best. On top of that, if you have work history gaps or have frequently changed jobs it will not look so good. In these cases, you should probably avoid this formatting style.

When writing a chronological resume, sections should be arranged in the following manner:
1. Contact information,
2. Resume introduction,
3. Professional experience,
4. Education, and
5. Additional skills.

If you're fresh out of grad school and don't have any professional experience just skip that section.

Functional Resume

The next resume writing style we'll break down is called a functional resume. Let's start with a disadvantage here: when reading a functional resume, it's hard for the employer to know exactly what you did in which position, and that will be a problem for some conservative interviewers. The reason I wanted this to be my opening line was not to frighten you, but to stress how important it to show your qualifications in the best possible light, so that your former job experience isn't that big of a deal.

Trying to hide the fact that you have imperfect work experience is the main reason to use a functional resume, because there are ways of how a functional resume can conceal your working gaps. What you want to do is to start a resume with highlighting your major skills and accomplishments in the past. If you have significant working gaps you don't want to draw additional attention to them. Instead you wish to speak about your qualifications and skills, to persuade the employer that you have what is needed to succeed.

Resumes made this way are a must for multiple career changers, and are very appropriate for liberal arts majors as well, for those with temporary positions or divergent careers, for those with wide range of skills in their profession, for students and for those who don't want to change careers entirely, as opposed to making slight shifts in the direction.

If you decide to go with the functional resume this is how the sections should be arranged:

1. Contact information,

2. Qualifications summary,
3. Relevant skills,
4. Professional experience and
5. Education.

Combined Resume

As you might have guessed, the combined resume is a mix of both basic kinds of resumes. Its purpose is to maximize the advantages of both chronological and functional resume, avoiding potential negative effects of either type.

This writing style is designed for job seekers who already have quite a bit of experience, but want to focus on skills and abilities right from the start. A combined resume is the best decision for those applying for a position that requires a lot of skills and expertise.

This format emphasizes your relevant skills, just like the functional, but still has plenty of room to provide details on your past work experience, like the chronological.

A disadvantage of this format is that it tends to be longer. You should write carefully and stay focused on the main skills and qualifications for which the job you are applying requires.

This is the order of sections in a combined resume:
1. Contact information,
2. Professional profile or qualifications summary,
3. Additional skills,
4. Professional experience, and
5. Education.

Chapter 3: Section Break-down

So far we were concentrated on technical matters and appearance of a resume, and now it's time to learn about the essentials. The know how of formatting and arranging your resume sections is very important for initial scanning and going through the first phase, but now you need to learn how to write about yourself.

How to present your skills, qualifications and experience are necessities. In addition, what are those marketing tips you need to use in order to get that interview call? In this chapter I will explain how each of the sections I mentioned before should look like, in order to make it easier for you to follow, I'll put brackets next to a subchapter title referring a specific formatting style. So, let's get to work.

Contact information

(Chronological, functional and combined)

The first section I will analyze is the one in which each formatting type begins: contact information. In contact information you need to include your name, address, phone number and e-mail. If you have a personal website, or LinkedIn profile you wish to add to your resume, this is the spot. Before adding anything that is not crucial for your resume, you need to ask yourself: "Is this important information that will impact my prospective job?" If the answer is "no" leave it behind.

Be cautious to check that your contact information is professional in appearance. You can't do much about your street name and address, but you can carefully scrutinize your email address. This is not the time to use your favorite address: PookieWookie@yahoo.com. If you do not have a professional sounding email address, get a new one just for job prospecting that says MyName@gmail.com. If you name is already taken, and you are named John Smith, for example, make your Gmail address reflect your profession. Use JnSmithEng, instead.

Make sure you list both your cell phone number and your home phone number on your resume. You want to be readily available when the hiring manager calls.
If you have voicemail, remove your background noises and record a new one with a pleasant tone and greeting. Make yourself smile while you record it; it makes a difference in the tone your prospective employer may hear.

Utilize your **LinkedIn** profile to make it work for you as an advertisement. Make sure it is up to date with all your good information, and eliminate anything that could be a detriment to your hiring opportunity. Have a great quality professional photo on your profile. More than 60% of hiring managers check the LinkedIn profile for appearance, professionalism, and contacts. If you are not part of a professional organization, join one on LinkedIn and contribute to the conversations. Employers want resourceful employees that are current on trends in the business world. LinkedIn has several ways that you can enhance your resume without spending a fortune on professional fees.

Resume Introduction

(Chronological, functional and combined)

A great resume must begin with an exciting introduction. This is your first, and maybe only chance, of getting attention from the recruiters reading your resume.
There are 3 specific types of resume introductions and in each format you'll need to use the adequate one.

The most commonly used introductions are:

1. Career Objective,
2. Professional Profile, and
3. Qualifications Summary.

All of these have the same purpose – to grab the attention of your potential employer, by highlighting your qualifications that are important, for the position for which you are applying. However, there is slight difference regarding the method in which they deliver this information.

For the chronological format you can choose between all three introductions, the preferred introduction for the functional format is Qualification Summary, and for the combined style you can use either Qualification Summary or Professional Profile.

Career objectives are great for people who are just entering the workforce or who only have a few years of experience.

Every career objective consists of three parts:

1. Years of work, or internship experience, and job duties performed.

2. Major qualities, skills, or abilities that you will apply to the specific position to meet the company's goals (you must be able to prove these skills in the professional experience section), and

3. Relevant degrees, licenses and certificates.

Be very careful when writing career objectives in a resume that will be scanned by an ATS, because you will have to use phrases that the system can readily identify. If you write them without any personal touch, the only thing you will accomplish is losing precious space, because the boring answers will get you discarded.

Many people, including me, think that it's impossible to write both meaningful and ATS friendly phrases so my advice to you is: avoid the career objective when constructing your resume so that you will stand out from the parade of job seekers.

A qualification summary is best for those people who have numerous skills or achievements they want to mention. This is the opportunity to shine with your enhanced skills and advanced professional training.

A qualification summary usually contains 5-6 bullet points that emphasize a candidate's:

1. Authority,
2. Creativity,
3. Recognition,
4. Efficiency,
5. Management, and
6. Communication.

The order of the bullet points is not determined by any specific rule, so it's completely up to you. It's always a good idea to start your listing with the most relevant and impressive point. This kind of introduction gives your resume a higher chance of passing through ATS software, as I mentioned before. Concentrate on relevant keywords and key phrases in your qualification summary.

The Professional profile is a mix of the best of both a career objective and a qualification summary.

This introduction should be based on four main points:

1. Years of experience,
2. Area of expertise or job duty at which you excel,
3. Transferable skills and
4. Career achievements.

Depending on how much experience you have you can include an additional point but it's strongly recommended not to go over five points or you will risk losing the attention of the hiring manager.

A good resume is not about including everything, but instead only including the relevant stuff.

Professional Experience

(Chronological, functional and combined)

Usually the work experience section is made up of a bullet point list of titles, duties, and responsibilities of each work position you've had in the past. However, in order for your resume to stand out, it's ideal to start the details of your work experience section with a powerful action verb. You should also use numbers to quantify your achievements because it looks more professional to hiring managers, than just a plain list of general descriptions of job responsibilities, and it gives a measureable result. I will now explain how to use action verbs and how to quantify your achievements in order to write the most appealing professional experience section.

You will always want to begin your bullet point details with an action verb rather than with a passive sounding description. A powerful action verb places you as an initiator of action, which leaves a good impression on the reader. Try to avoid starting off descriptions in a passive manner and use action verbs instead, for example don't say "responsible for" but rather use an action verb "managed". Have in mind that you can find lists of those action verbs you can use all over the Internet, so if you have problems rephrasing some sentences, those lists can be really helpful.

In addition to action verbs, I can't stress enough how important it is to quantify your achievements when writing professional experience section. What does that mean? Employers want to see workers who can achieve solid results and those results are best presented in terms of reportable numbers. How many employees did you work with or oversee? How much of a budget did you work with? By what percentage did you increase sales or efficiency?

You need to use numbers in detailing your work experience, in such a way that you demonstrate that you are results-oriented rather than task-oriented, and every single employer is seeking measureable results. Including such numbers in your professional resume make it easier for the potential employer to get a defined idea of what you have accomplished. In order to measure your accomplishments, try to obtain as much data as you can in regards to your work experience, but you should never make up numbers. You also don't need to quantify every single line in your work experience, but if you have those numbers. Don't be afraid to use them!

Education Section

(Chronological, functional and combined)

You already know where you should put your education section, based on which resume format you decided to use, and now it's time to learn how to write one. Unless you are a student or a recent graduate, your education section does not have to be too detailed. Usually it's enough just to write the name and location of your university, type of degree and date when you graduated.

However, if you are a student or a recent graduate, your job experience section will probably be thin, or you could not have it at all, so the education section has to be moderately detailed.

The education section can have a lot of variants depending on which level of education you have, whether you are still in school or recently graduated, did you have any job experiences at all, and so on and so forth, so I will try to explain what is necessary for you to include for whatever that your specific situation.

First of all it's important to list education in reverse chronological order, degrees or licenses first, followed by certificates and advanced training. Set degrees apart so they are easily seen and bolded. Whatever you think is your most impressive accomplishment should be stressed.

You may wish to include a coursework synopsis, the core purpose and findings of your senior research projects, any abroad or independent studies, publications or awards from your education experience. Additionally, you may include some reference to your contribution to college expenses through part time or summer employment and scholarships. Include every formal or informal experience you have that is related to your job application, and if your major or overall GPA is 3.0 or above (on a 4.0 scale), you may wish to include this information also. GPA information is usually only shown for the first job search after college and is generally dropped from the resume after that.

Relevant Skills

(Functional)

Relevant skills section is the core of writing a functional resume. It is really important to choose at least three skills that are significant for the job for which you wish to apply; if you can list more than three do so, but don't include anything that's not applicable to the job position you are pursuing. For each of those skills you should come up with 3-4 bullet points that help provide evidence of your abilities. Just like in professional experience section, it's a really good idea to add numbers, so that your potential employer could see that you are able to fulfill the requirements. Aim for at least one quantified bullet point for each skill. You want to avoid using phrases that aren't grounded with some personal experience; your employer needs to see that you are truly capable of implementing skills you claim to have. You need to be precise and direct and rest assured that it would draw the employer's attention.

Additional Skills

(Chronological and combined)

Apart from relevant skills you wish to emphasize when writing a functional resume, there are sets of skills you can include when writing a chronological resume, and absolutely have to include when writing combined resume. Don't get confused by the adjective "additional" because you should only include skills applicable to your desired job. However, in additional skills section you have more space for skills that are not directly related to the position for which you are applying, as long as they are relevant. For example, if you are applying for an assistant manager position at a music shop, it's acceptable to mention if you play an instrument. It isn't primarily related to management but it shows you have knowledge and interests about the industry.

When listing additional skills try to keep this section as organized as possible by grouping similar skills. Like before, it's always a good idea to add numbers that will define your skills and make them more receptive to your potential employer.

Chapter 4: Tips that Will Help You Get Started

Now that you have acquired the knowledge you need to write a brilliant resume, I want to give you a few tips that will help you go through the initial phase of writing, as well as reviewing your finished resume. In this chapter I want to create an imaginary scenario that will help you prepare for an actual job seeking.

Let's say that you've found a job opening that perfectly fits your personality, your ambitions, qualifications and most of all, your desires. You feel like you were meant to get that job, and you wish to send your resume as soon as possible.

The first thing you have to do is to put yourself in the position of the hiring manager who is going to read your resume and decide whether you are the right person for this job.

Do Research

You need to ask yourself: What would make me the perfect candidate for this job?

If you are seeking a job in a field you know well, you probably already know what would make someone a superior candidate. If that's not your situation, you can always gather hints from the help-wanted ad you are answering, you can talk to your friends or acquaintances who work in the same field, or even better, in the same company. You could even call the employer and ask them directly what they want. Don't make any wild guesses, it is very important to do this step thoroughly. If you are not addressing your potential employer's real needs, be sure that they will not respond to your resume.

You have to think about what the employer really wants, what special abilities would a potential employee have to have, what set of skills and experiences are relevant to that specific position, in short: What would distance an exceptional candidate from a good one?

I suggest that you write that question on a piece of paper and then brainstorm all potential answers you can think of. Take all the time you need to thoroughly examine that topic in search of possible answers. Write everything down, even things that don't seem so relevant in that moment; you will determine later on what should stay in your resume and what shouldn't.

The main idea is to loosen up your thinking so that you will be able to see some new connections between what you have done and what the employer is looking for. When you finish brainstorming proceed to the next step.

Make a Plan

Now that you have made a rough draft of your resume, you should go through the answers you listed previously. Prioritize answers, based on which qualities or abilities you think would be most important to the person doing the hiring. At this point you should start thinking about what resume format will be the perfect fit for your resume. If you have problems determining which format is the best one for you, try to write all three of resume introductions and see which one you like most. With the knowledge you now have regarding resume writing, your first initial assumption will most likely be the best fit.

Write Your Resume

When you've made all the decisions you should start writing your perfect resume. Think about all those important things you've read about earlier in the book. List only important and relevant data, highlight your desired information, double check for spelling and grammar errors, make your resume both reader friendly and ATS acceptable, stay focused and direct. While you are writing your first resume give yourself a little space for tryouts, it would be a good experience to write more than one resume.

Review Your Resume

After you write your resume, leave it for a few hours and then read it. Try to put yourself in a position of a hiring manager, read it just like he is going to. That means that your first reading shouldn't take more than one minute. If you are not satisfied, and you probably won't be, correct parts that you have problems with and read it again. Repeat this until you're finally satisfied and excited with your resume. You shouldn't need more than 5 repetitions to achieve that goal, but if you are still not satisfied, don't panic. If you think of yourself as a highly self-critical person, you should give your resume to someone else.

Even if you are satisfied with your work, having someone else to review your resume is extremely important. Make sure that you give it to someone who will actually tell you if something bothers them, a friend that will tell you it's good so you wouldn't feel bad is probably the wrong person for that job.

Use the Internet

I didn't talk much about researching on the Internet until now because I wanted you first to understand what resumes are, so you could make your own picture of how one should look. Now that you have knowledge, you need to spot the difference between a good and a bad resume; it could prove helpful for you to search some resume examples and practice the role of a hiring manager. Bad examples can help you in this phase, because if you are able to spot a mistake in somebody's resume, chances are you are not going to make that mistake yourself.

Also you can find lots of lists of keywords and phrases that will be useful for writing yours.

Chapter 5: How to Refresh Your Resume

I want to dedicate the last chapter of this book to a future you. I will provide you with some useful tips on how to keep your resume shiny all the time. Although I hope you have managed to find your dream job already, it's always a good idea to keep your resume up to date. You never know if or when you are going need it. Basically, you have to change your resume in both directions. At least once a year you should add some new spectacular things you've done, and also remove those parts of sections that don't represent you the way they did. Your career is on a path of constant progress, so your resume should be able to follow that path and reflect your professional growth.

Adding New Employment, Skills and Accomplishments to Your Resume

Refreshing your resume means keeping it current. If you've changed jobs during the past years, maybe earned a promotion or expanded responsibilities, it all should be stated in your resume. After some years on the same job, you've surely mastered some new exciting skills, or you have new great accomplishments: all of them should be written in your resume.

If you are thinking about a career change, you should probably make some radical moves and adjust your resume to the desired position.

Add professional-development activities you completed last years, including certificates, degrees, new courses you've attended and in-service training. Also include professional organizations if you've joined some. List all of the training programs you've begun, even if you haven't completed them. This shows your commitment to ongoing professional development.

Removing Old and Redundant Information

As you add new valuable information, you will need to remove any old and redundant data that isn't representing you the way you wish. You should always have in mind that the resume is not your biography, so information that was valuable few years ago doesn't have the same power anymore. Although every job experience you have is important for you as a person, you don't have space for all that in a resume. For the end of this chapter I wish to repeat that advice I've been trying to give to you through the whole book for the last time: Stay focused!

A Final Note

Thank you for downloading my book. I hope that this has been a source of value for you and is able to help you land that job you've always wanted. I have helped many people through getting their first jobs, changing their career direction and leaving work altogether! I can guarantee, if you use the guideline set out in this book, you will be successful in no time at all.

Despite resumes and cover letters being indispensable in the process of hiring, we cannot turn a blind eye to platforms such as LinkedIn. Many recruiters and employers say that LinkedIn is their number one resource for recruiting and hiring new employees. To help my readers, I have also written a book on how to use LinkedIn to attract recruiters – it's available on the Amazon store, take a look!

Finally, if you enjoyed this book and it provided value to you, I would really appreciate it if you could leave me a review on Amazon.

Wishing you all the best,

A.J. Robbins.

Made in the USA
Charleston, SC
08 February 2016